BOOK OF DREAMS
Mervin M. francis

© Mervin Francis 2024
Book Of Dreams
978-0-6398518-0-8 – Paperback 2nd Edition
978-0-6398518-1-5 – eBook 2nd Edition

Published by SAKURA BOOK PUBLISHING - South Africa
alta@sakurabookpublishing.com

All rights reserved. No part of this publication may be reproduced, stored in a retrieval system, or transmitted in any form by any means electronic, mechanical, photocopying, recording or otherwise without the written permission of the copyright owner.

Cover Design by Micaela de Freitas
Printed in South Africa

I dedicate this book to my loved
ones, who encouraged me to
follow my passion and turn
this dream into a reality.

And I give thanks to the Heavenly
father for blessing me with
the amazing gift of poetry.

POETRY

Poetry is the expression of emotions
controlled by the heart
It shows off your feelings right from the start
Like a songwriter whose life is within a song
Those cherished memories, both right and wrong.
Such are the words put down on paper
Of plans for one's dreams, or even just a caper
Some bring tears of joy or pain
And some enter the heart to forever remain.
But most of all, they bring much love
To those that are blessed from the heavens above
Uniting the dreams and making them one
So that life together will be a lot of fun.

I DREAM OF YOU

I dream of starry nights and summer's sighs
Of cloudless skies and pigeons' cries
Of gurgling brooks
And your lovely looks
Of happy times that we both share
And the endless love in our hearts laid bare

I dream of sweet, scented flowers
And of spring's many showers
Of chirping birds that on tree tops play
And what our horoscopes have to say
Of love and happiness that is so great
And those things I know that could never wait

But most of all, I dream of you
Of places to go and things to do
For us, our love was created
And never to be separated
Through happiness and sorrow
And the times we may borrow

And now that you know how I feel
I hope that this dream will one day be real
And we can show the world that Love Really Rules

MY LOVE

My love is like a butterfly
A feeling I know that will never die
Cause you are the one that is so sweet
That gives my heart that joyful beat.

A love that makes my feet to swing
That showers my life as though it's spring
Cause you are my love, my world, my all
That makes my life a splendid ball.

And if you had to change your life
I'll dare not have you as my wife
Cause you are so wonderful as you are
And you will forever be my shining star.

That shines so bright within my heart
And with this feeling I'd dare not part
For all the riches in the world.

A PRAYER FOR YOU

Heavenly Father full of grace
Bless this lady's pretty face
Bless her heart that flutters when we speak
Keep her safe, humble, and meek

Bless her hands that are so strong
May her happiness be lifelong
Bless this girl I hope to marry
Bless my child I hope she will carry

And if she hears this Prayer of mine
Bless those thoughts that enter her mind.

HEART'S JOY

As the Sun rises to bathe the earth with light
May it forever in your heart shine bright
As the wind blows through the open space
May it make you smile as it caresses your face

May this new day that we now see
Grant your heart much joy to roam so free
Like a dove in flight in the skies so high
Such freedom it has as it passes us by.

As you enjoy this beautiful new day
I wish for your happiness, come what may
Love, joy, and laughter forever more
In your life, I know you will always store.

I LOVE YOU

My love for you runs so deep
And I dream only of you as I go to sleep
I allow my thoughts to roam so free
And cover my eyes but still I see

For you were everything my heart desired
And now that you're gone, I feel so tired
As though everything from within has been drained
And I've been left out in the rain

I feared that this day would one day come
And now that it has, I know not, what can be done
But still I dream that we'll be together
And if we don't, I feel I would wither
For one thing I know that is so true
It's all because "I Love You"

SCENT OF FLOWERS

As sweet as the scent of flowers
My love for you turns to showers
And gently falls around my thumping heart
Which allows my lips to slowly part

To send out words that caress my thoughts
Like some of the things that cannot be bought
And puts my head into a spin
Like a boxer thumped hard on the chin

But to know that you are not around
Makes me feel as though I've drowned
And brings tears to my lonely eyes
Which makes me feel like I want to die

I will not give up on my struggle
To get you back, and me out of trouble
For you are the one that I love and adore
You are the one that my heart beats for
Now and always, your love forever more.

NAUGHTY BUT NICE

Life is a breeze, so they say
Enjoy this life, come what may
For life is an adventure waiting for you
So embrace this life with everything you do.

Naughty but nice
And as cool as ice
Short and sweet
And knows how to turn on the heat

Hotter than a blazing fire
More dangerous than a gun for hire
So love me or leave me or take what you get
For believe me when I say: you ain't
seen nothing yet.

I LOVE THEE MORE

I love thee more than words can say
I love thee more with every day
I love thy sweetness and smiles so bright
I love the peace at the end of a fight

My love for thee shall remain the same
As my love for thee is not a game
For I love thee through my aches and pain
My love for thee shines bright like a flame

I know that my love for thee is great
I'll show thee more when on a date
For I am more alive when we are together
And in thy arms I will remain forever.

YESTERDAY

Yesterday has come and now it's gone
While tomorrow is yet to be born
Now today is here and forever will stay
And that's the truth, come what may.

We look up at the skies in wonder
Is there really a Heaven that awaits us yonder?
What dreams do we dare to open our hearts to
Which challenges to face and what should we do?

Questions are asked of this life that we live
Answers to all, I hope we can give
For this life that we are given on earth
Is a challenge we face right from our birth.

WHAT WEAKNESS

I wish I knew the reasons why
My head goes in a spin and my heart leaps high
What is this magic that surrounds this girl?
That has caught my eye like a beautiful pearl

I'd often sit and stare
At this maiden so beautiful and so fair
To speak to her, I'd often try
But words would not come as she passed me by

What is it about her that sends me tripping?
For when she's around me, my strength starts slipping
And a sudden weakness takes over me
I wish I could speak to her and set my heart free

Free from the spell that she has over me
The one that's clouding my head so my eyes can't see
Grant me the strength to take the lead
To tell her I love her, yes indeed.

I WATCH THE SUN RISE

I watch the sun as it brings a new day
As it warms up the earth in a special way
How much of joy it brings to one and all
Embrace it and take heed to our hearts' call.

Jump with joy as we open our eyes
Dance to the tunes as we hear birds' cries
Reach out to the ones that brings you joy
Embrace life's gifts like a child with a new toy

For the pleasures of life are gifts from above
Made for you and sent on the wings of a dove
Accept this special gift and make it your own
Hold it tight like a king on a throne.

FRIENDSHIP

A friendship so fine, a friendship so rare
Losing this friendship, I never would dare
For a friend like you is one in a million
Oh, I do mean one in a trillion

One so sweet, strong, and gentle
A vision to me that is unforgettable
I give thanks to the one that brought you here
To brighten my days and remove my fear

This friendship I've found,
Helps me keep my feet on the ground;
Take on the world without looking back
While it keeps my head held high and always on track.

Thanks to your friendship so true
Thanks for making those grey skies blue
Thanks for the thoughts and support all day long
Thanks for the encouragement and for
making me strong.

I DREAM ABOUT A STAR

I dream about a starry summer's night
That is brightened by the pale moonlight
As I sit on the shore staring into space
Thinking of the life and beauty of this place

Oh, what tranquility the world has in store
As it opens our hearts to love some more
As we embrace the moments of what we shared
As we open our hearts to the ones that cared

As night yields to another beautiful day
I thank God for whatever comes my way
And as the sun covers the earth with light
I look at the sky and embrace that awesome sight.

TRUER WORDS WERE NEVER SPOKEN

Life is too short to dwell in the past
Life is too short to keep coming in last
I thank God for the strength bestowed upon me
To take charge of my life and the world to see

Life is too short to stifle one's dream
Life is too short to accept things as they seem
So from this day forth I take charge of my life
I lift my head up high and walk away from my strife...

With God by my side I am armed
His blessings keep me safe from harm
For his words are my road that I will travel
From this day forth never will I grovel

LOVE IS A FEELING

Love is a feeling that is so true
And the things we've done are new
And the life that I've lived was so dull
And now that we've met, my thoughts are full

My life is great, and far from hell
As the time will be, when we shall dwell
Together forever and ever to come
Together forever and one we'll become.

AS THE MUSIC PLAYS

As the music plays all day long
My heart breaks out into a song
Words automatically spring to my lips
As the music teases my hips.

Oh, how sweet life may seem
Am I awake or is this a dream
For I feel like I'm lost in a maze
No wait, I'm sitting alone in a daze.

With a smile on my face I look out yonder
Warmth in my heart like a spell I'm under
Oh, what joy I feel stirring deep inside
And now all this joy I dare not hide.

MY PLEDGE

Three words I pledge to you my dear
These words I'll say when you are near
Words so sweet and gentle
Words that are so sentimental

They bring great joy to one and all
And dissolves life's problems great and small
It adds sparkle to the darkest night
Creates hope and makes everything bright

It adds its spice to every dream
Brings togetherness and creates a team
These three words that I have pledged
Make life exciting and puts me on the edge

These three words that I must say
Are words that take me through every day
That bring joy to my heart, and the skies stay blue
Are the simple words "I Love You"

MY DEAR FRIEND

May the blessings from above fall upon you
May He always make your grey skies blue
May all your wishes and dreams come true
May joy and laughter fill your heart too

But most of all, I wish you love
And may it be blessed from the heavens above
These blessings I pray will fill your heart
And when joined, may they never be apart

So have a nice day, my dear friend
For love and blessings to you I send.
And may they help your heart to mend
And may it always be filled with a joyous blend
So take comfort in these words to you I send.
Now and always, may your happiness never end.

STARS IN THE SKY

I love you more than the stars in the sky
I will love you truly 'til the day I die
For you are to me my world and more
These feelings my heart will forever store
I may not be the perfect being
But from this love I'm never fleeing

I love you dearly, I love you true
I love you forever, no matter what you do
So come on, girl, and walk with me
Show our love for the world to see
To have and to hold 'til the very end
Walk beside me, my love, my best friend.

MOMENTS IN TIME

Fleeting moments are all that we share
Fleeting moments catch us unaware
For time is the one thing that's never on our side
It rushes by like the ocean's ever-changing tide

Moments of truth that we hold so dear
Moments of love that shine so clear
How do we embrace these moments so sweet
To allow two hearts to dance in joyous beat

A moment in love is an eternity for some
So embrace that moment and the love that comes
Make every second feel like an hour
And make your love rain down like a shower
To soak in her heart for a lifetime and some.

SLEEP

As I lay my head on my pillow to sleep
I think of dreams of us I'll keep
Of times that we have shared
And all the happiness and care

And as I close my eyes to sleep
I feel a pain in my heart so deep
For I miss the scent of your sweet smell
And your arms wherein I could dwell

Beside you, girl, is where I want to be
To share our love and set our feelings free
So we could express just how we feel
And sit at times and enjoy a meal.

HAPPY BIRTHDAY

Happy birthday to you, with love
May this day be blessed from the heavens above
A lot of things I would like to say
Like I wish you the best on this special day
With tender love, hugs, and kisses
May they all come true, your birthday wishes

LOVE ALWAYS

I will always love you
And that, my girl, will forever be true
No matter what people have to say
That's the way my heart will always stay

Be it day or be it night
My love for you will always shine bright
There will also be pain and sorrow
But trust me, girl, it will pass before tomorrow

For this love I have in my heart so deep
I plan to forever keep.
To help me to see the world so bright
And this love will forever be my guiding light

SPRING IN THE AIR

Look up, look down, and then look all around
Sit back and listen to the earth's beautiful sounds
Of chirping birds in the skies so blue
While the earth's flowers are covered in dew

Is it just the magic of spring in the air?
Or the earth that is covered in its natural flair
That brightens our lives and opens our hearts
Like a flower in bloom with its petals apart

So sit back and listen with your heart and mind
Sweet things, believe me, around you, you will find
So think of this and smile away
Should ever something try to spoil your day

BY MY SIDE

I feel all strange, deep inside
These feelings for you, I will never hide
For the love I have for you
Is oh so sweet and true

It gives me great strength and hope
And with any problems, I find it easy to cope
Just knowing that you are there by my side
And one day for sure you will be my bride

Until that special day comes along
To you my heart you will always belong
And all that you will have to do
Is to return my love and keep it true

And from this love that we share
Our hearts will forever have tender love and care
And all the pleasure that our love will bring
Our hearts shall with joy sing.

HEART'S DREAMS

All my dreams are built around you
And my love for you will forever be true
I know not what the future will bring
But I will do my best to make your heart sing

Sacred are the dreams that come from the heart
And nothing on this earth can tear it apart
For love is the king that rules this throne
And such is my heart that could never turn to stone.

There comes a time when we all must learn
To stem the tide and allow your love to burn
For it's fueled with love and happiness
A thing so powerful and filled with greatness
To guide our lives, our hearts, and dreams
To courageously show what we really mean.

ESPECIALLY FOR YOU

You walked into my life a total stranger
At first I thought that I was in no danger
But as I got to know you more
Then I knew that I was not so sure.

You seem to have opened up another door
The one that I seem to have been longing for
One that has been closed for far too long
The one which has stored my heart's special song.

What have I done to meet someone like you?
Those in this world that are so few
One so sweet, and yeah! So cool
So please tell me if I'm a fool.

For there is something about her that has changed me so
Given me strength and joy to get up and go
And if I ever have to lose this friend
Then this heart of mine will never mend.

A SMILE

Oh! What a smile you have displayed
It made me think of a game I once played
Enough of that, I heard myself say
Cause just looking at you has made my day.

How sweet you looked just standing there
It made me think what fools we were
To ruin the love we felt for each other
All that, just to please another.

As time has passed and wilderness tamed
My love for you remains the same
I should fear what the future brings
But knowing you're there allows my heart to sing.

BEST OF LIFE

The beauty of living is to live
The art of fighting is to win
The sweetness of singing is the song
The brightness of the sun is its rays
The wisdom of life is to age
The dullness of time is the night
And the best of life is to LOVE

A NEW DAY

How do we feel on this beautiful sunny morn?
A day filled with sunshine and smiles is being born
A day to be merry and a day so bright
A day that is full of heavenly light

So, take a look around and enjoy the view
For this day for all is still so new
Embrace the fact that you are here to see
Enjoy the fact that your thoughts can roam free

Take in and enjoy this beautiful day
Forget the past and embrace today
Smile and dance for the world to see
Let your heart sing and roam so free

The journey begins with a beautiful new day
Open your mind in a positive way
Challenge yourself to lose all fear
Absorb the feelings and hold on to everything dear.

FEELINGS

This feeling I have is so very strong
A feeling I know that can never be wrong
Although these feelings sound so strange
My love for you I will never change

The ways of life I used to live
That showed me things I didn't believe
Since you came into my space
The challenges of life I'm ready to face

One day at a time I hear myself say
Take on the world, come what may
This feeling within has made me wise
Now forward I go with my eyes on the prize.

BROKEN DREAMS

Many dreams are sometimes broken
When to your loved ones, wrong words are spoken
And when you are alone, you sit and wonder
What is this spell, your love is under?

Now if you express just how you feel
Then broken hearts will quickly heal
But if we tend to ignore their pain
A beautiful romance could go down the drain.

You would never really see
Just how beautiful love could be
How much love you could have displayed
So in your lover's heart no sorrow would have stayed.

WEDDING MARCH

As you walk down the aisle with your daddy
Holding hands, walking towards me
So much love in those eyes
Girl, that's all that I can see
So much love for you and me.

I plan to share my life with you
Forever, I promise to be true
'Cause you are the only love for me
And in my heart, there's only you

So, come join me now at the altar
Where our vows together we shall take
And the blessings from above
Shall shower upon our love
And make it strong, this love within
Make it strong, this love indeed.

'Cause together, that's where we belong
And forever, I pray our love stays strong
Cause I love you, with all my heart
Right from the very start.

TIME SLIPS AWAY

I sit here thinking while time slips away
Of what lies in store for this beautiful day
Thoughts of children running so free
Carefree smiles are all that I see.

Enjoy every moment as we embrace this day
Make them count, come what may
Dance with joy as your heart sings
Hold on to the happiness that it brings

Reach out to the serenity that engulfs you
Breathe in the joy and happiness too
For life is a blessing sent from above
Take it all in and share all your love.

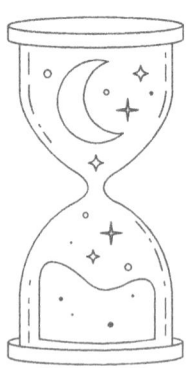

I MISS YOU

Oh! How I wished for these days to go by
For I missed you dearly and that's no lie
Though you were constantly on my mind
My heart would wander as though it was blind
In search of something that was always there
And at your picture I would always stare.

I know our love has made me strong
'Cause it showed me exactly where I belong
No matter what we have to face
Our love is deeper than the empty space
Be it day or be it night
Our love will shine forever bright.

So do not fear when I'm not around
'Cause toward you my heart is bound
So remember, girl, when you are feeling blue
No matter what, I will always love you.

ON MY MIND

Yes, there is definitely something on my mind
And as I search I know what I will find
Someone who is sweet and caring
Someone who is free and sharing

Who is not afraid to take a chance
To see life through as though it's a dance
I often think of what will become
Of this beautiful girl that plays so dumb

Well that's the way I guess life starts
While at this moment we are apart
But one day soon I pray and hope
With the troubles she carries her heart will cope

The strength that she needs, she will find
And the love that she seeks is not left behind
So stick around and we will know
How our love will one day grow.

INNOCENCE OF A CHILD

A baby's laughter always rings true
It turns darkness to skies of blue
Brightens up the saddest of days
Bringing us joy in many of ways

The look in their eyes, so pure
For all sickness, the cure
One look would chase all the frowns away
Their innocence and mesmerizing styles,
I wish will always stay

Hold them close, hold them dear
For the joy they bring is abundantly clear
Embrace the time as they start to grow
Love them dearly and forever let them know
That they are loved

OPPORTUNITY

Love is a beautiful dream
Which is more than people make it seem
Some say it's good and others say it's not
But together it's quite a lot
When opportunity strikes, do not wait
Take that chance and go out on a date
Enjoy what you have while it's there
For once it's lost, your life will be bare

Follow your heart to where it may lead
Take that stand and follow your needs
I know at times it's a lot one can ask
But if you do, it becomes a meaningful task
Just as long as you are not sad
Enjoy life and don't get mad

Feel free if you may
And don't go astray
Cause if you wish, I may lead
We'll be happy, yes indeed
So don't you worry
Cause you will be sorry
If you miss out on such an opportunity

BEAUTY WITHIN

How beautiful is the sky on a cloudless day
How sweet is the music that nature has to play
That brightens the earth with joy and laughter
And makes Mother Nature our ever after.

How sweet is the message that enters our mind
How sweet it is to those that are blind
Who listen with their heart and soul
And the feelings they get never grow old

Now take it in with a breath of fresh air
Absorb it in your heart if you dare
Hold it dear and never let it go
Trust in nature and she will teach you all
you need to know.

THANK YOU, GIRL

A breath of fresh air is what you are
You will forever be my shining star
Who stands by me through thick and thin
Who is never afraid to thump me on the chin.

As life throws us problems left and right
With you by me side, I'm ready for the fight
No matter how rocky the storms may be
Your encouraging words bring strength to me.

So watch out, world, as I am on my way
To challenge myself, come what may
You see, I'm stronger than ever before
The world's my oyster and I am in search for more

So thank you, girl, for standing beside me
For helping me grow and my strengths to see
And as I make this forward move
Thank you, girl, for helping me find my groove.

WORDS

Words cannot express how much
you mean to me
For words cannot say much, you see
What I feel is hard to say
Nor will it end with night or day.

For blessed was I to find a love so true
To show me happiness and a life so new
No actions, girl, can make matters turn
And the love within can make sorrow burn

It strengthens dreams, hope, and love
With all that comes from the heavens above
And now that we are together again
I realize that you have taken away my pain

With your happiness and smiles
I watched heartache die
While love triumphs through
its splendid miles
And while the doves in the winds cry
For me you will always be my heart and soul.

AS THE SUN RISES

As the Sun rises to the greet the earth
As the birds sings and makes us alert
To the changing of time from night to day
So flutters my heart in every way

With thoughts of you that dance in my mind
And scare me senseless and makes me blind
What did I do to deserve this beautiful lady
For being away from her drives me crazy

I pray that she never tires of me
I pray that her beauty a lot more I get to see
I hope that my heart is filled with her love
I hope that this relationship fits like a glove

May your day burn bright
And your darkness find light
And in your heart love is never out of sight.

A DREAM

A gentle breeze caresses my face
Like a tender kiss with all its grace
I close my eyes and start to dream
Of a beautiful place near a silver stream.

I look up from my dream at the sky above
And what do I see: a beautiful white dove
Soaring gracefully through the clear blue skies
Without any care, just a chirp, and off she flies.

I wish that life was so carefree
With joy & serenity for all to see
And so much better this world would be
And then I awaken to reality.

ABOUT THE AUTHOR

Mervin M. Francis is making his debut in poetry. Mervin lives on the North Coast of Kwa-Zulu Natal, South Africa.

His boyhood dream was to write poems for Hallmark, but adulthood saw him in a career with Toyota SA.

Mervin still continues to write poetry, and his poems are about the love in his heart and the joy of the world around him. He has now decided to publish his work so that he may share it with the rest of the world.

www.ingramcontent.com/pod-product-compliance
Lightning Source LLC
Chambersburg PA
CBHW042343300426
44109CB00049B/2823